I0505799

A Field Guide to the Workplace Jungle

© David Avery, Jacqui Hogan and Ron McIntyre 2015

© (Animal cartoons) Jacqui Hogan

No part of this book may be reproduced in any form, without prior permission in writing from the copyright owner.

First published 2015

How often do you find yourself thinking of your workplace as a jungle or, if you are less exotic, the local forest?   The conversations and actions that take place seem to be very reminiscent of any number of animals that you may run into strolling in the wild. Sometimes those conversations or actions can be comical and sometimes they can be shocking.

This book will give you some ideas for making your journey safer, more enlightening and fun.

Contents

Introduction

How often do you find yourself thinking of your workplace as a jungle or, if you are less exotic, the local forest? The conversations and actions that take place seem to be very reminiscent of any number of animals that you may run into strolling in the wild. Sometimes those conversations or actions can be comical and sometimes they can be shocking. That was the idea triggered when we embarked on our book, 'Together Works: The Ultimate Guide to Effective Collaboration'.

The animal illustrations we referred to in Key 2, 'Dance the Group Dynamics', have become one of the most discussed sections so we decided to embark on taking this deeper down the path into the workplace jungle or forest. We will allow enough flexibility in our examination that the practical tips can be adapted in any physical or virtual workplace, factory or institution.

When was the last time you took a walk through a forest, wilderness or jungle? Like most of us who are city dwellers, the chances are that you may not have done the jungle route but everyone has made a trip to the forest or some defined wilderness, even if it is through a wilderness park.

Initially, we were going to refer to the 'Workplace Menagerie' as our examples included both domesticated and non-exotic wild animals. We considered that a number of our readers would have little to no experience with the exotics, and we looked for alternatives that could cross various experiential or cultural barriers with ease. We looked at forest, the wild, wildlife park, zoo and others, but we finally settled on the term 'Jungle'.

Rudyard Kipling's *The Jungle Book* (1894) portrays a number of animals as metaphors for human society. He showed that the 'human jungle' is not lawless, but based on intricate assumptions and expectations of behaviour.

Since the objective of our text is to look at a brief comparative of certain animal behaviours with people behaviours in the workplace, calling our workplace a jungle seems entirely appropriate.

As we walk through the workplace jungle each day, critters of all sizes, temperaments and personalities surround us. Some are like small cuddly animals that we love to hold and cherish while others are ferocious and animated. Some make our walk enjoyable and comforting while others make the jungle miserable and confrontational.

To help everyone enjoy his or her walk, we decided to create a practical Field Guide for walking safely through the workplace jungle.

According to Wikipedia, the definition of a Field Guide is a book designed to help the reader identify wildlife (plants or animals) or other objects of natural occurrence (e.g. minerals). It is a guide designed for you to bring into the 'field' to help distinguish between similar objects. Field Guides help users to distinguish animals and plants that may appear to be similar but are not necessarily closely related.

It will typically include a description of the objects covered, together with paintings or photographs and an index. More serious and scientific field identification books, including those intended for students, will probably include specific, hallmark keys to assist with identification.

This will be a way of identifying workplace critters and learning how to deal with them from interaction to avoidance. Our hope is that this whimsical, walk through the Jungle, will provide a fun insight to attitudes and actions that can either enlighten or dim our daily work environment. The key to this Field Guide is that the examination starts at home, with ourselves, because we are not immune to being affected in some way. How many times are we the cause of our own problems so it really is critical that we remain open and flexible when using this guide?

Background

In 2007, Stanford professor Robert Sutton wrote 'The No A—hole Rule: Building a Civilized Workplace and Surviving One That Isn't.' This was really an examination of what kind of 'jerks' existed in the workplace and how to tolerate them.

This made Sutton an expert on the behaviours that seem to infest every workplace. He points out that they are more than just a nuisance; these people cost companies money.

"Since the book was published, there has been more and more research by academics and there are more and more cultural reason to believe the cost might be higher than we previously thought," he said. "There's more evidence of turnover and more evidence that if you are around a boss or co-workers who, after dealing with them, leave you de-energised, you're less likely to work hard, you're less likely to be creative."

Many companies have begun screening job candidates for 'behaviour' tendencies, making it clear to employees that respecting others is paramount to how they are evaluated.

Even with this simple start 7 years ago we still have a long a way to go in understanding the workplace as both a physical office as well as a virtual environment.

In the book, we attempted to make sure that everyone understood that the technology was NOT the silver bullet for engaging employees to become more productive and supportive of the organisation where they work. In our opinion, the core for building engagement is based in the relationships and processes that are jointly agreed to and acted upon within a team, group or enterprise.

To make this more fun we are going to borrow some insight from animal behaviourists. Animal behaviourists study the way animals behave and try to determine what causes certain types of behaviour, limits to interactions between species and what factors can prompt behaviour change. They usually specialise in certain types of animals, whether it is fish, birds, large animals, wild animals, livestock or household pets. They also may focus on certain types of behaviour, such as hunting, mating, or raising offspring. We are going to specialise in the 'business' animals whereby we compare some animal behaviour with human factors and extrapolate some comical parallels.

Many things can influence how an animal behaves, including hunger, illness, hormones, the presence of a potential predator or prey, even the weather. Animal behaviourists identify behaviours and try to answer key questions about them, including:

- What caused this behaviour?
- What factors influenced the behaviour?
- Why did the animal perform this behaviour at this particular time?
- How did the animal learn the behaviour -- or is the behaviour innate?
- What purpose does the behaviour serve?
- Does the behaviour change over time?

We will examine similar influences as they apply to our work environment. There will be those that are very positive influences on the organisation while others will have a negative impact on teams, groups or enterprises. It is important to note, we can all be affected by these attitudes, behaviours or feelings if we are not aware of what causes them. With this in mind, we must really understand that any identification with a type of animal and someone you know or work with is purely one of a generalisation. It should not be used to make judgments but rather to guide us on how to adapt and flex our behaviour to allow for consistent and productive relationships, regardless if they are in person or virtual.

What will we examine?

Our jungle will contain some of the animals from Key 2 of Together Works but in more depth and colour. We will also include some additional residents that may be beneficial to understand. Generally, we will look at information categories that follow, however the format of each section may vary:

- **Description:** The name - 'Angry Alligator' for example. The special characteristics of the animal and its environment, that influence its behaviour. .
- **Identification in the wild:** how does this animal behave in the 'wild' environment? What type of environment feeds or limits the power of this species? What types of influences can this species exert over other species that they may relate to or fear?
- **Identification in the workplace:** how does this animal behave in the workplace? What types of responses are in the quiver of this species, both positive & negative? How to spot this particular behaviour in the workplace.
- **Tips:** how to approach, benefit from, work with or avoid the outcomes of this behaviour.

You will note that we are only looking at behaviour types that we can either manage or lead, not specific ailments or characteristics tied to an individual. Our approach to this topic is going to be one of **IF IT MAKES YOU LAUGH, IT IS GOOD MEDICINE!**

So, without further ado, let us open our Field Guide and take a fun, lively and challenging journey or safari, your choice.

How adventuresome do you feel today?

Eurythmic Enabling Elephant

Coordinating, Skill Sharing

Elephant Description

African elephants are the largest surviving land based mammalian species, growing to 4 meters and 15,400 lbs (7000 kgs). Asian elephants are only a little smaller. They have a unique physiology, with a large trunk used for both breathing and lifting objects, including water. An elephant's trunk is actually an extended nose, which they use for drinking, lifting objects, and making sounds as well as smelling and breathing Elephants are mega herbivores, consuming as much as 330 lbs of plant matter every day. This, combined with their large size, requires them to be persistent and generalist feeders, sometimes clashing with farmers as a result

Both male and female African elephants and male Asian elephants have tusks, which males use when fighting. Unfortunately, these ivory tusks are highly sort after and we have decimated the world population of these gentle giants.

Elephants have few predators - lions, tigers and other predatory species tend to keep their distance.

Elephant behaviour in the wild

Elephants are highly social creatures with a well-developed and complex range of social interactions. When greeting each other, they develop and maintain their bonding through touching and rubbing together. Younger elephants play together constantly, looked on by their older and well-respected elders.

Their society is hierarchical, with the older females at the apex, where they are deeply respected and listened to by the rest of the elephant clan. A clan can consist of as many as 100 individual elephants. You can almost imagine the deep and meaningful conversations about experiences being shared between the older more experienced elephants and their younger members of the clan. The young elephants listen intently to the complex stories told by their elders, as the sun goes down and the world, and they, prepare for another day.

Elephant society is also matriarchal, with females taking a strong lead in how their society works and functions. This is not to say that bull elephants do not have a place, but that females determine what is and is not acceptable behaviour.

Elephants are not particularly territorial, being nomadic in nature. They move from place to place, eating steadily as they go. Their physiology is not designed for them to stay in one place which is why you may see them swaying back and forth when constrained e.g. in a zoo.

Elephants are slow moving and deliberate in their movements. Nevertheless, like many large animals, they can be relentless and destructive without realising.

Elephant behaviour in the workplace

Elephant behaviour can be found in almost all workplaces, although it is not particularly commonplace. It may seem more commonplace, because those with this preference change jobs often. Many highly respected consultants and mentors will be inclined towards elephant behaviour, as their experience, altruism and consistency are valued and shared amongst many people. Having an elephant on the team can be very beneficial to any organisation.

Elephant behaviour is usually seen in very experienced members of the team, members of which will see them as the main source of how things are done in your workplace. They will be highly respected and a natural place for people to go to in absence of other firm leadership. They are natural leaders. However, their style is not the front-of-the-pack outspoken way we often expect leaders to be, but more of a deeply respected oracle. Elephants have long memories. You may find that your team members will check your decisions with the workplace elephant before they implement them. Like their animal counterparts, they have a deep sense of moral justice and sense of fair play. They are extremely trustworthy and reliable.

There will be no exhibition of ambitious behaviour, but they will step in as leader to ensure continuation of the team, if necessary. They are not territorial so, provided everything is going well, they will not challenge the existing leader.

Elephant team building behaviour is eurythmic (harmonious), sophisticated and valuable for creating the high levels of trust and skills exchange needed to enable highly functioning teams. It will also help with creating collaboration between teams. Elephant behaviour is non-threatening, which helps the team to trust them first, moving on to learning to trust each other through mutual support, communal information exchange and shared protection from predators

You may also have heard the expression 'The elephant in the room'. Sometimes elephant behaviour can hold you back, if not dealt with promptly. Their relentlessness can be very destructive when dealing with someone without the vision to appropriately apply their knowledge. However, although you know you need to deal with it, it is a potentially huge problem.

Tips for dealing with Enabling Elephant behaviour

1. If you are fortunate to have an elephant on your team, it is wise to bring them close to you and learn what you can from them, while they are there. They will be knowledgeable and willing to share; they will appreciate your respect, and your team will respect you too.
2. Utilise their behaviour to create strong teams and cross collaborations, but also create a supporting infrastructure to maintain these once the elephant has gone.
3. Value their loyalty, by giving them your support.
4. Do not just 'remove their tusks' and leave them to die a painful death. In other words value their knowledge as a whole, holistically, do not just suck a piece of it and discard them.
5. Because elephants are so good at creating strong team bonds, you need to make sure that their purpose aligns with yours. If not, they may become 'The elephant in the room' – impossible to ignore, but a potential source of great difficulty to deal with.

We now move from our coordinating and skills sharing elephant to another unique animal type, the Gingerly Giraffe. Here we see an animal that is strategic and careful about its surroundings.

Gingerly Giraffe

Strategic, Careful

As the Giraffe pauses to take a well-earned meal from the very top of the highest acacia tree, with its huge eyes it looks out over the distant horizon. The Giraffe's eyes are the size of tennis balls and miss little. It sees a very distant lion prowling and, although the lion may not be coming this way, decides to flee somewhere safer just in case. With long and powerful legs, it lopes across the vast plains of the Serengeti, where it knows it can run fast for a long time. Those long legs together with the Giraffe's massive heart allow it to propel itself at a heady 30 miles an hour.

Prey animals, like zebra and antelopes, will watch for the fleeing of Giraffes. They know that this means danger is approaching. Wise animals stay nearby Giraffes, using them as a sort of early warning system.

Giraffe Description

Giraffes are large and very impressive animals. They have large eyes and a long neck, making it an animal that is hard to ignore. It has the largest eyes of any mammal and its long neck enables it to see at a heady six meters above the ground. This enables the Giraffe to see further than almost any other land animal. Although its camouflage and running speed enable it to flee danger, it is its long-range vision that enables it to see danger well before other animals.

Giraffes communicate infrasonically – a very low pitch - which most animals cannot hear; until quite recently, scientists thought they were actually mute. Giraffes also use their eyes and body to communicate.

Being a very large animal, the Giraffe has a greater requirement for water than most. To drink it must squat down with splayed legs and bend its neck to the ground. In this position, it is very vulnerable to predators like Alligators. Fortunately, the Giraffe has a greater ability to conserve water than even a camel.

In mythology, the Giraffe is sometimes associated with the Chinese Qilin. The Qilin is a mythical horned and hooved creature that appeared only in lands ruled by a wise person. It is a creature that helps good people and pursues wrong doers. Many people believe it is a symbol of prosperity, success and luck, which is ironic, because the gambling, drug dealing and prostitution industries still fear the Qilin in China. Until the explorer Zheng He[1] brought a Giraffe back from East Africa (via Bengal) early in the 15c, the Qilin was often depicted as a unicorn or dragon headed ox. Zheng declared that the Giraffe was the legendary Qilin. The Japanese still use the same word 'kirin' today for both the Qilin and a Giraffe.

Because of its unusual appearance, many people thought the Giraffe was a myth along with creatures like the giant squid and Komodo dragon. In Greek mythology, it was sometime called a Camelopard - a merging of a camel and a leopard. The Giraffe is still a great favourite in zoos around the world.

Giraffe behaviour in the wild

The Giraffe is not territorial, preferring loose associations with other Giraffes. While curious, they are naturally cautious and will flee rather than confront danger. Although they may appear to be gentle giants, if challenged and they

---

[1] Zheng He was a famous Chinese explorer, treasure hunter and admiral of a Chinese fleet of over 300 huge ships during the Ming dynasty. According to some sources, he was seven foot tall, a Eunuch and a Mongolian Muslim from the Yunan province. He was, and still is, revered in China for his extraordinary voyages. Some people claim he discovered North America almost 70 years before Columbus.

cannot run away, a Giraffe can be quite ferocious. Although they can do you serious injury with their huge powerful necks, or shatter bones with their large, hard hooves or just by falling on you, they rarely do.

In the zoo, they can seem sad, almost pitiful creatures. Confined to small pens, they have little opportunity to see or travel long distances. Giraffes are such gentle and pleasant creatures that they are often overlooked or taken for granted. Only on the open spaces of the grass plains, can you truly appreciate these magnificent creatures in their full glory. Few sights more impressive turn from the trees and run majestically across the dirt track in front of you. Giraffes are quite curious, and will stop to see what you are doing. They will poke their heads inside your jeep, confident in the knowledge that danger is still far away. There is a sense that they are always gathering information, sifting it and calculating whether this changes the danger status.

Giraffe behaviour in the workplace

In the workplace too, Giraffe behaviour needs freedom of information to scan the long-range forecasts and make their predictions of danger. They also need decision-making freedom to lead out of danger. It should be said that this is not leadership in the sense of being charismatic, extrovert or outspoken. It is just that people trust this judgement and so they follow where the Giraffe leads.

Although they can appear isolated and lonely, they are equally comfortable in small groups or alone. They do need space and freedom to act, however.

Because this constant visual grazing can look like uncertainty, you are unlikely to find workplace Giraffe behaviour in fast moving environments or those with high degrees of change. Instead, you are more likely to see this behaviour in larger, safer organisations, where the rest of the team appreciate long-range vision and there is time and space to act.

As Stephen Berry says in his book, Strategies of the Serengeti[2] 'The Giraffe's combination of height and exceptional eyesight give it an unequalled advantage when compared to other land animals. These two areas of competitive advantage create a situation where all other aspects, including its speed and lack of dependence on regular water intake, are subordinate to the Giraffe's vision'.

The ability to scan long-range, adds to the strategic nature of Gingerly Giraffe behaviour. This preference for gathering long-range forecast information, competitor information enables better prediction of trends and identification of opportunities. This, combined with an innate caution, also

---

[2] Strategies of the Serengeti by Stephen Berry – a look at different approaches to strategy in an environment where getting it wrong is literally fatal

encourages small adjustments in their position to avoid the need to run away.

You have may have already seen this behaviour, although this is not always easy to spot immediately. Giraffe behaviour does not usually include the ostentatious preening exhibited by other workplace animals like the Ostrich. While this may appear to be introverted and passive, Giraffe behaviour is focussed, cautious, pragmatic but always ready to act.

Like the Giraffe in the wild, there is a quietness to their conversation that can seem like an unwillingness to communicate. This is not the case. Giraffe behaviour is more about what they do than what they say. A Giraffe behaviour preference means you will need to observe actions and query more - building a communications bridge that helps you interpret the danger, they sense in more detail.

Another way to recognise Giraffe behaviour is in the way people who feel more vulnerable will congregate around them, safe that a calm and unconcerned aura means they are safe. As in the wild, the Giraffe sense of confidence attracts people with less understanding or vision of the future, as they know that they will have advance warning of trouble coming and time to act accordingly. There will be no manipulation or domineering - just a natural attraction to safety.

There will be no sense of territory and no involvement in workplace politics. There will be little involvement in short-term trivia and day-to-day tactical behaviour either, just a general attraction to a goal of safety. People can believe that what they say and do is truly impartial.

It is easy to misunderstand Giraffe behaviour because of its calmness and apparent lack of communication. There is no bravura, so this can appear like unexpected action taken for no apparent reason, especially when the rest of the workplace sees 'nothing serious'. However, make no mistake, if you see someone exhibiting Giraffe preferences take defensive action – the danger is quite real.

For most people, Giraffe behaviour means alertness and foresight, prudence and safety. There will be an appearance of aloofness perhaps, but any rapid change will be a good barometer for major dangers.

Tips for dealing with Gingerly Giraffe behaviour

1. Take advantage of this talent for seeing the long-range strategic picture. Although it is primarily a danger-focused vision, it may well give you a sense of the urgency of certain risks. You may even be able to use this vision to help you sort through alternative strategies going forward.
2. Expect to make extra effort in your communications. Take time to ask questions and listen to the responses as this will give you access not only to all the accumulated knowledge, but also the insightful conclusions that may help you understand your risks and assess alternative actions.

3. Give your team access to a wide range of information so that those with Giraffe tendencies can sift this information for what is relevant and useful.

4. Be aware that your team may prefer to congregate around the more cautious Giraffe behaviour because it feels 'safe'. Whilst it is helpful to have this long-range perspective, it is a cautious one and may make it more difficult to make innovative changes that have a high degree of uncertainty associated with them.

5. Keep an eye on any changes in behaviour that indicate a tendency to run. You will need to respond quickly, either to run fast or better understand the situation and calm the behaviour.

From here, we move on to the Observant Owl, which is aptly named because it can be very agile and generally unflappable when dealing with its environment, let us "hoot" on then.

Observant Owl

Alert, Unflappable

Everyone has a story or two about the hooting owl. Some of the stories are positive and some of them are negative but everyone has an idea of what an Owl is all about. We find similar people in our workplace jungle so we need to come to grips with the owl. The perception is that they are wise, scholarly and extremely observant but unfortunately, the opposite is true.

Owl Description

Owls have been a fascination for humans for centuries. Much human behaviour is attributed to Owls in history. There are cave paintings that show Owls as primary focus. There are some 205 varieties of Owls from around the world so it is a very familiar bird to most people. Owls are predominantly nocturnal in nature with some varieties being more active at dawn and dusk however, the eye adaptation is key to this feature.

Owls have a unique facial panel that houses large forward facing eyes and ears. This face panel is flat with a set of feathers that helps emphasis the lines and picture that is referred to as the facial disc. Some Owl facial disc can be very reminiscent of a human face hence the fascination we have had with them over the years.

These feathers also provide another function in that they can be adjusted to help focus sounds that come from various distances onto the owls' ear cavities. Those ear cavities allow for some extremely acute hearing abilities.

Owl behaviour in the wild

The uncanny hearing is extremely sharp and helps the Owl to be vigilant and on alert when others seem to be resting. We often hear the term 'Hoot' or 'Who' when dealing with the sound of an Owl but in reality the familiar hoot is usually a territorial declaration, though not all species are able to hoot.

Other sounds Owls might make include screeches, hisses, and screams. Owl vocalisations are loud and low-pitched. Their cries travel well through the night air, enabling them to locate mates and declare territories despite the darkness.

Most birds have eyes on the sides of their heads, which gives them limited depth perception. For them to see anything to the side they must turn their heads to see. On the other hand, the Owl has binocular vision due to the large frontal facing fixed position eyes.

Owls are farsighted, i.e., they are unable to see clearly anything within a few inches of their eyes but at distance the eyesight is very keen and sharp. Their eyesight is also extremely sharp in low-light situations. Physically they have small 'feelers' on their beaks and feet that help them manipulate the close in prey or activity.

Physically Owls can rotate their heads and necks as much as 270 degrees due to a difference in the neck vertebrae between them and other species. The smallest Owl species weighs in at approximately 1oz and measures to 5 inches. The larger Owls can approach 10 pounds and reach a length of 28 inches with a wingspan of 6' 6".

The wingspan coupled with some very specific function feathers, allow Owls to fly almost silently so with all the other attributes they are very effective at hunting.

Owl Responses

In terms of intelligence, the Owl is not the sharpest tool in the box. They have a tendency to be dim-witted and require repeated attempts at certain activities. This lack of innate intelligence drives them to be very methodical and logical in all they do. They are not big risk takers.

Socially they are family orientated and they can be territorial. The have strong talons to not only kill its food and eat but also to defend the nest, if required. The average lifespan of an Owl is between 10 – 20 years. As adults, they will spend a lot of time preening themselves using their beaks and their talons, which have some very specialised combs attached.

Owl behaviour in the workplace

Owl behaviour in the work place is typically identified as a wise individual who has the demeanour to be calm and very aware of the surroundings. Generally, they are able to create early warning signs for various activities that may occur and warn others, similar to the Gingerly Giraffe.

In this particular activity, they are similar to the Meerkat, just not as active. Generally, the Owl behaviour is a good attribute to a team because they will be protective of the group and warn the group to upcoming dangers. Like the owl, this behaviour is usually perceptive in terms of seeing opportunities far out but generally lose sight of those things happening directly under their noses.

Generally it is social but can be very territorial and make loud voices to defend his or her protected area. It will not be the centre of attention within the group and will choose to be quiet in terms of day-to-day movement within the group. The person with Owl behaviours will be very observant in what goes on in their group and will often be accused of having eyes in the back of their head. This is not a risk taking behaviour so the actions will be cautious and deliberate. It will love a structured and methodical approach to doing something the same way every time. Once the person with this behaviour finds a home or family, they will be reluctant to change, choosing rather to protect the group and its territory.

Tips for dealing with Observant Owl behaviour

1. Understand that Owls can be solitary in nature. They will work within a group but they will also treasure their own time with little interaction with the other team members. This can be hard to deal with if the leader is looking for continual communication in the group.
2. As with the owl, who is nocturnal, Owl behaviour is often not found in a morning person. The behaviour will lean toward starting later and working later than many on the team. This ties together with the solitary nature described above and may take some adaptation from the leader and other members of the group. Allowing for flexibility will keep the Owl behaviour happy and productive.
3. The environment needs to allow the behaviour to have a wide territory to survey and grow. This allows it be become a very positive participant in the team. Like the owls, the groups cannot be very populous nor can there be a large number of Owl behaviour people in the same group. This means that leaders must be aware of the attitudes and support for the behaviour.
4. Knowing that Owl behaviour patterned people are not risk takers by nature means that the leader provides some protection for them. The more standardised the job or processes they are working on, the better for both

the individual and the group. They will be very observant and listen carefully when engaged so this can be beneficial to any active group.

Moving to the next animal takes us from the Observant Owl to the Minimal Mouse. This animal will face various levels of criticism and praise depending on your point of view. We offer up that they reflect a humble yet clever and persistent attitude. Without further ado, we can scurry off.

Minimal Mouse

Humble, Clever

Description of the Minimal Mouse

The Mouse is one of the most under-rated and interesting creatures in our workplace jungle. Because it is diminutive and cuts a low profile, its value and importance are often overlooked. Its behaviour is not just survivor behaviour, it is thriver behaviour, and given half the chance, it will thrive in most situations. No house is Mouse-proof! Or, as the song goes, "There's a Moose Loose in the Hoose!"

Aesop's Fable of 'The Lion and the Mouse' shows the humble little creature gnawing through the rope net that has trapped the mighty beast. This reminds us of how useful the Mouse can be in clearing obstacles and constraints with its ineluctable application to small but important tasks. The efforts of the Mouse cannot be dissuaded or resisted and, frankly, why would we want to? Let's face it, in the workplace, the Minimal Mouse is one useful little critter.

The Mouse was venerated In Ancient Greek mythology as an avatar of Apollo[3]. It was known as Mouse Apollo. The temple was a home for mice, beneath the altar a Mouse nest, with Mouse symbols on the altar. The Greeks even had coins with the figure of a Mouse on them, sometimes depicted nibbling an ear of corn.[1]

This mythical Mouse is one of a global range of semi-socialised animals known as the trickster archetype. (Others include the rabbit, coyote and spider. Think Mickey Mouse, Bugs Bunny, Spiderman, Anansi and Wily Coyote.) The animal archetypes that share our homes but not all our rights or responsibilities actually signify the semi-civilised semi-wild child, it can apply to people of any age but it always signifies an element of semi-exclusion, youthfulness or immaturity.

---

[3]http://www.online-literature.com/andrew_lang/custom-and-myth/6/

The Argives, according to Pollux, {110c} stamped the Mouse on their coins. {110d} As there was a temple of Apollo Smintheus in Tenedos, we naturally hear of a Mouse on the coins of the island. {111a} Golzio has published one of these Mouse coins. The people of Metapontum stamped their money with a Mouse gnawing an ear of corn. The people of Cumae employed a Mouse dormant. Paoli fancied that certain Mice on Roman medals might be connected with the family of Mus, but this is rather guesswork. {111b}

Mouse behaviour in the wild

Mice are very adaptable and will go wherever the pickings are richest. Most live in fields and forests, but our focus is those that live in proximity to man, for it is the impact of Mouse type behaviour on human systems that concerns us.

Commonly regarded as a persistent pest, the Mouse is an unwelcome guest in most houses. Despite its diminutive stature, it inspires fear, dread and even panic. They have foo-dar (food-radar) to sense a hearty meal even through walls and will gnaw through plaster, wood, cardboard and paper to reach it.

Because they are so small and so unwelcome they tend to be extremely shy of people. They feel constantly threatened and often rightly so for many of even the most tolerant animal lovers would gladly see them exterminated. They are great at hiding in wall cavities, behind skirting boards and so on; if you should catch sight of one, they are almost impossible to catch alive.

Mouse behaviour in the workplace

Mousy behaviour can best be described as timid but persistently industrious. It may display elements of outsider-identity, but will always retreat from confrontations rather than defensively standing its ground.

This behaviour can sometimes be despised, not because it is verminous or germ-ridden, but for its humility and shyness and its tendency to skitter away from conflict. It tends to hide away and is happiest when left unnoticed to gnaw slowly and surely through the knotty problems others may have neglected or discarded; it might seem like small stuff or even detritus if you are not inclined to be mousy, but it is a juicy morsel to get your teeth into if you are.

Anyone who feels like an outsider may commonly display minimal Mouse behaviour, avoiding others and just getting on with things quietly. A person acting like this needs to be more thoroughly integrated into the social arena of the workplace. They may need your help to get there. This may call for sensitive cultural awareness if the 'outsider' feeling involves ethnic, age or gender difference.

It is not necessarily that we naturally exclude those who are different, but their feeling different can make them behave in a mousy way which is then disliked for being out of step with the norm. This is a common scenario leading to fear and loathing of those who seem mousy.

In general, Minimal Mouse behaviour should be met with nurture and appreciation. Every hero started out as a trickster, and the quiet little Mouse has qualities of greatness we find in some of the greatest animals in this book (including the dour determination of the donkey, the ineluctable tenacity of the Terrier and the positive disruption of the Chimp), but all in such an unassuming way that there is something quite charming and endearing about it.

We see Minimal Mouse behaviours in every workplace, and when you see it, remember its great value as seen in Aesop's fable. Honour the Mouse among you. It punches way above its weight and is a useful critter to have around in lots of ways.

Tips for dealing with Minimal Mouse behaviour

1. If you manage someone who acts mousy, you can be assured that they will work ceaselessly and with a high probability of success on even the knottiest problem. Assertiveness training might help them if that is an option, and possibly cultural awareness training for others if appropriate. Also, you can set up situations that will encourage them to act socially with others in a group and try to build confidence and understanding to break down barriers that way.

2. If your boss behaves mousy, they must be a true master of their field, for they were not promoted by aggressive competition. Watch and learn! Another good thing is you do not have to worry about being bullied.

3. If a colleague is mousy, be reassuring in your actions, showing that you are not a threat. Be welcoming. They could turn out to be your most loyal friend.

4. If you recognise some Mouse behaviours in yourself, you may need to make a special effort to show yourself and share your good work with others. Remember the lion's best friend is the Mouse, and even the elephant is scared of it. Be in your power and don't hide your light!

Now from this relatively humble animal we move on to the equally humble yet visibly hard working Eager Beaver. Very enthusiastic and industrious the Beaver is usually a good model for others. Off a building we will go.

Eager Beaver

Enthusiastic, Industrious

The Beaver wakes from his rest, consumes a good breakfast and prepares for the day. He is looking forward to an active day of cutting down trees using only his sharp teeth, floating the resultant logs along the river and then adding them to the carefully constructed dam. There he will carefully place them, crisis cross fashion to produce an intricate structure that is both strong and beautiful. He expects to be working diligently all day. That is, unless a threat appears in the form of a bear or other large animal appears. Then he will warn his Beaver teammates be smacking his tail loudly and forcefully on the water surface before diving deeply to safety. He will stay in his chosen place of safety until he is sure the threat has gone, then return to his work and continuing where he left off, until it is time to rest and sleep.

Beaver Description

Beavers are herbivores and prefer to eat roots, plants and leaves. Their teeth continue to grow throughout their lives, meaning they must continue to chew food and wood to keep their teeth at a manageable size. They do not hibernate, and stay active all year round, creating the (correct) impression that they are eager to work and are working constantly.

While Beavers are large and ungainly on land, once in their natural habitat of water, they are smooth and graceful. Beavers are able to swim at up to 5 miles an hour and stay underwater for up to 15 minutes without surfacing. These traits make the Beaver ideally suited for building dams on rivers and streams, and their homes or lodges in the resulting pool.

Beaver behaviour in the wild

Beaver families consist of monogamous pairs and their young, which the adults raise jointly. Beaver families can be quite large, requiring regular extensions to their lodges. When the young leave the family, they tend to settle quite close by. They are territorial, and can be quite intolerant of intruders who do not belong to their extended family. Otherwise, they are not generally aggressive, despite those very sharp teeth, preferring to escape and return when the danger is down.

Being ideally suited to their environment, Beavers are specialists. They work to dam rivers and brooks, cut down trees and create ever more elaborate Beaver lodges for their expanding families. This can transform large areas of land and forest, bending them to the will of the Eager Beaver. They can have a huge impact on their environment, because they are able to manipulate their environment like no animal other than man. There are differing views as to whether this is positive or negative, but there is no doubt as to their impact. They are limited to waterways however, and have been decimated by human hunting for their fur, castoreum secretions and because they compete with man for land.

Beavers play a variety of roles in Native American folktales, from the diligent, persevering hard worker to the selfish, stubborn creature. Images of the Beaver can be found carved in totem poles throughout the US. The Beaver is the stuff of which legends are made.

Beaver behaviour in the workplace

It is not even dawn, and the workplace is deserted except for the Eager Beaver. They are the first person in the workplace every morning and the last person to leave in the evening. If they are not there, it is only because they took the work home.

You will often see Eager Beaver behaviour in the younger specialist or recently joined. They may be single or divorced as all the work, work; work that they do leaves them little time for a social life. Nevertheless, they do not really mind.

Eager Beavers often form the backbone of the team, as they prefer action to talking, and are able to work in a focussed way for extended periods. They do not seek accolades for what they do, so are often forgotten. They do not shout to the world "look at me, aren't I wonderful" like an Ostrich does.

They work equally well on their own on a project as in a team, although prefer to work with other Beavers. They are likely to see less focussed team members with suspicion and intolerance.

Once their goal has been set, they are very task focussed, and pursue those tasks relentlessly. They are highly motivated towards activity. Sometimes they are over eager to get going, and forget that sometimes a little review before action is necessary. They are reasonably creative, provided the problem is not too unusual and is a clear obstacle to their goal.

Diligence in the pursuit of their 'to-do-list' is a mark of Eager Beaver behaviour in the workplace. They are one of very few that actually finishes the tasks on their to-do lists! This diligence makes those who behave this way, reliable administrators. This behaviour means they will follow the process to the letter. This focus is so strong, that it often excludes the sideways vision needed for good management, although it can be a helpful trait in specialist areas e.g. IT consultants, scientists etc. With a Beaver on the team, things will be done.

The downside of this behaviour, and a major weakness, is that they do not see the big picture and are blind to the impact their task has on other tasks by other people. This means that they do not take into consideration what the impact of what they do may have on the tasks and activities of other members of the team.

This focus can also make it difficult when dealing with a major change, as it may make it difficult not to just back to the task. If the change requires a different task, Beavers need additional time for you to explain and change the new processes and tasks involved. Once you have assigned them a new task however, they will pursue this as relentlessly as before.

Tips for dealing with Eager Beaver behaviour

1. Explain how their tasks fit with the overall goal, and remind them at regular intervals. Make it clear what you want them to do and any restraints they must work to.
2. While they do not need close supervision, you should keep an eye out for potential impact on other teams and team members, because they will pursue their goal relentlessly.
3. Although they do not need a great deal of motivation, it is easy to overlook their development. A "thank you" will probably only elicit a brief nod of the head, as they do not really like to be interrupted.
4. They will probably prefer a quiet space in which to work. A workplace with other people milling around provides too much irritating distraction.

5. Manage change carefully. People with a Beaver behaviour preference will make assumptions that are not necessarily in line with the overall goals.
6. Try not to overload them with work just because they are willing!
7. Make time go review progress with them; they are unlikely to come to you if they get into difficulties, but their solutions to problems may not be in the best interests of the team as a whole

I hope that you can see there is some merit to the Eagar Beaver but now we move on to a beast of burden, the Devoted Donkey. A Donkey is really a focussed animal that can be very involved with its own group. Let us trot on then.

Devoted Donkey

Enduring, Focussed

Did you know that the Donkey (or ass) was the next animal, after the dog, that humans domesticated for work and they were the first to do agricultural work?

Because of its unique association with humans, the Donkey seems actually to like human beings and to enjoy working for them (when conditions are right; otherwise, it does no more than consent). It is one of the most intelligent of the animals that humans use for work.

Generally, Donkeys are gentle animals, which make them particularly suitable for being worked by women, at least in those parts of world where women are predominantly responsible for farming.

A happy, healthy Donkey is one that will do most work for its human owner. If it is not healthy, a Donkey cannot give good work. Housing and feeding contribute to their health, so are just as important as the more direct care and prevention of ailments and injuries.

Description of a Donkey

At 250 to 650 pounds, Donkeys are smaller than most cattle, mules or horses and may not be able to generate as much pull as those aforementioned; however, Donkeys are stronger and work twice as hard as cattle. Donkeys can pull carts faster than oxen on well-maintained roads, however not all roads are well maintained.

The way to get the best work from Donkeys is to have them worked as a pair. Generally, a relationship develops between the pair. Any separation from its friend may cause Donkey unhappiness, and permanent separation may even cause it to die of heartbreak. This tendency to friendship and pairing is, therefore, both an advantage and disadvantage.

The primary tool in training Donkeys is the human voice. The donkey's ears are very acute, and even though it does not understand words, it is excellent at comprehending personalities and moods. When working with donkeys, therefore, a human must talk as much as possible.

Key point to remember about Donkeys is that each one has its own personality and preferences; each Donkey is unique and different from every other. They easily recognise different people and know their ways. Owners should, in turn, easily be able to recognise different Donkeys and know their habits. The Donkey is an animal that forms decided habits.

The Donkey is one of the most rewarding animals to train, and once trained can be trusted to do many tasks without human supervision. A Donkey will learn quickly both from other Donkeys and from humans, and has a remarkable memory, especially for paths and routes.

Environment of a Donkey

A Donkey has the ability to adapt to many environments. This is evident by the wide range of habitat where they can be found e.g. helping farmers plough fields, carry loads and pump water etc.

For work in irrigation type farm situations, oxen are generally better suited than donkeys. There, soils are heavy and saturated with water which, combined with high humidity, make this environment uncomfortable for donkeys.

A Donkey matures slowly and should not be used for work before it is 3 years old. A very well cared-for Donkey can live beyond 50 years and give useful work for about 30 years.

It is the needs of the farmer that will decide which characteristics are most desirable, and what further training may be done. Some of the characteristics, such as speed and obedience, are often the outcome of training a Donkey before it is old enough to be used.

To some extent, a Donkey will select itself. An owner will often know what kind of work his or her Donkey will like doing best and be best at. A buyer should not choose a Donkey until they can see it regularly in use. A donkey's temperament can often be judged by the way its owner handles it.

Since Donkeys often work in pairs, they should, if possible, be chosen in pairs. A pair of Donkey friends will do better work.

Largely, a donkey's temperament can best be assessed by spending time with it and working with it. For example:

A Donkey with a calm temperament would, in an open field allow a strange human (or donkey) to come quite close before moving away. Then, when it does move, it will move slowly.

Likewise, a responsive Donkey will be very observant and, allow a stranger to come close in an open field but it will be prompt in backing away from any odd or unusual movement.

On the other hand, an excitable Donkey will run, probably kicking its heels in the air, when seeing a stranger in an open field.

Finally, a good working Donkey should be obedient; this means the Donkey knows the commands and responds to them quickly.

Especially for carting and carrying, the Donkey must be nimble and not be clumsy. It should be able to turn round in a space only a little wider than itself and able to climb up and down a gentle set of steps.

Of course, a Donkey will not understand the meaning of most of the words said around it, but there is a range of words and sounds that a Donkey can easily be taught to understand and associate with actions to perform. Such words or commands should be standardised in any area.

The presence of any other well-trained Donkey makes it much easier to train a new one.

There is no doubt that Donkeys learn as much from each other as they do from humans.

Devoted Donkey behaviour in the workplace

Devoted Donkey behaviour in the workplace is a lot like its animal counterpart, they are an intelligent and hardworking member of many teams in the workplace. They can usually be counted on to work well with others and not be distracted by too many different influences around them.

Also similar to the Donkey a healthy, engaged human is one of the primary assets of any business. They are valuable and worth spending the money to train and maintain them in positions of trust and loyalty.

Just as their counterparts, this behaviour can be counted on to work better when they are paired or teamed together thereby creating a unit. If you match your Donkeys well, they will be extremely focused and driven to provide excellence for the company.

Many of the characteristics that we talk about in the environment of the Donkey will be similar to the existence of the behaviour in the workplace. The temperaments highlighted above can be replicated in the human counterpart behaviour very easily with similar reactions.

For example, calm Donkey behaviour can be very trusting and obedient whereas excited Donkey behaviour can exhibit a level of paranoia about its environment and constantly be looking over their shoulders. The key is that how they are trained and empowered drives this attitude. If you ignore this group, you have no one else to blame but yourself.

We have no doubt that the workplace Donkey behaviour will learn as much if not more from its fellow associates than it will from any formal training that may be offered by the company. They will be supportive of each other and strive for the good of the group.

Tips for engaging Devoted Donkey behaviour

While there are many similarities between an animal Donkey and the requisite workplace behaviour, the focus should be the same in either case. The goal is to maintain the productivity in the situation so that it can grow and permanently establish itself in the environment.

1. Remain consistent when speaking to and engaging with a person exhibiting the Donkey behaviour. They will respond to the words but more importantly, they will respond to the actions, moods and attitudes that the leader exercises.
2. Strive to ensure that this behaviour is able to connect with other team members to be productive and sustainable. There are a number of tools that can assist with this process including a DiSC assessment, for example.
3. Remember that like the donkey, each person exhibiting this behaviour has a unique personality with all that accompanies that recognition. They will have their own preferences, likes and dislikes. Their values, perceptions and goals can help a leader assist them in growing.
4. This behaviour's ability to learn and adapt will vary. There is no cookie cutter method for teaching new processes or engaging then in knowledge growth so having an understanding of the triggers that drive each person can be very beneficial to encourage growth.
5. To ensure that someone with this behaviour maximises their potential it is best to observe them in various situations and with various associates. Typically, there will be an indication of comfort and willingness to listen

and grow when allowed to interact for a period. Keep your eyes and ears open during this process.

While the Donkey can seem laid back and focussed, the Meerkat Monitor can display hyperactive behaviour but they also provide models for collaboration. They also develop cliques. Heads up, let us see who is coming.

Monitoring Meerkat

Collaborative, Cliquey

As we open the office door, we are usually aware of who is active in the room and who is seated depending on how the cubicles or offices are set up. It can be very interesting if you have, a cube farm with low profile cubes because then you can see the Meerkat Cliques at work:

- Who pops up every time something happens within earshot?
- Who is watching the doors if there is a group conversation taking place?
- Who scurries to the cubes when the boss comes into the room?

- During normal break times, does the cube farm look like a game of whack-a-mole?
- Is the vigil one of preservation, group preservation, or selfishness?

Meerkat Description

Meerkats (*Suricata suricatta*) belong to the mongoose family. Generally, the African desert dwellers form close-knit societies composed of up to fifty Meerkats. Unlike their relative the mongoose, who chooses to live solitarily, Meerkats are known to have some of the most cooperative societies. They inhabit all parts of the Kalahari Desert in Botswana, South Africa, and Mozambique.

Meerkat, like many in the animal community, communicates in three ways, visual body language, sounds and scents. We would have trouble trying to interpret what a Meerkat was trying to communicate is we saw one approaching us screeching and flopping limbs because we don't understand meerkatese, it may be trying to intimidate you or trying to distract you so the others could get underground.

According to Animal Planet, the Meerkats have an extensive vocabulary; for example, they purr if they are content, they will chatter if they are nervous and they will squeal if there is danger. They also have sounds that they use when trying to organise food foraging and surrounding threats such as a snack. In short, the communications of a Meerkat are usually staccato and to the point based on need or function.

The Monitoring Meerkat

A helper or a non-breeder generally performs the monitoring role, i.e., one who is keeping vigil. They are on the lookout, watching for possible predators and other potential threats to the community. This position rotates amongst different members of the group in no particular order or structure. They are usually around when the group is away from the burrow looking for food. The Meerkat on the lookout will sound an alarm by producing a distinct bark. This allows the young to flee inside the burrows and under protection of adults. Some experts have constructed theories based on kin selection or reciprocal altruism; while the Clutton-Brock paper mentioned above proposes simply that, the individual's optimal activity is to be on guard once its stomach is full.

Selfish Guards?

The role of the guard had been thought to be altruistic for quite some time before Timothy Clutton-Brock (1999) published research that proposed Meerkats who take on the role of guard (He refers to them as Sentinels) are actually doing so in order to serve their own interests. Their selfish behaviour may be the group's redeeming quality as a whole, because the sentinel is still responsible for alerting others who may be busy searching for food to the presence of predators. This selfishness hypothesis rejects the general notion of the altruistic guard, and does in fact provide a foundation for later research that in turn has produced further theories concerning motivation behind guard behaviour.

There is a model that suggests that guarding individuals are selfish because instead of being costly to the guard, it is actually beneficial to them. Clutton-Brock supported this model when he found that guards actually have lower predation risk than food seeker. They actually provided evidence that the guards position themselves at safe sites. For example, the guard on average stays half the distance away from the safety of their bolthole. Therefore, when the food seeker on average is over three meters away, the guard is slightly more than 1.5 meters away. Being this much closer to the bolthole gives the guard an advantage over the forager, who has to travel a longer distance to reach safety.

What is a Meerkat monitoring behaviour?

This particular behaviour is usually very subtle and can be both beneficial and negative depending on the situation. It is not a dominant behaviour except in extreme situations where there is a constant fear within the workgroup.

First of all, groups are not all bad, the cube environment can provide a protective home for individuals in large open enterprises, if required, but at the same time one must be aware there is some self-driven motivation which may become an issue.

This person's behaviour may be part of their role in the organisation since they will generally be in a supportive role rather than front lines, similar to the Meerkat. This supports the protective nature of the behaviour but it will also allow them the ability to use this role to their benefit. They will not be the first one to deal with or point out a potential problem within the product or service but they will alert if there are human threats within the group.

Meerkat workplace environment

A Meerkat monitoring behaviour usually displays itself in people who have a tremendous feeling of justice and wanting to protect the group. They will seem like jack-in-the-boxes when there is activity going on in the workplace. They will stand up often just to see who is moving and try to ascertain any potential threat that may be approaching. They will seem to be focused on helping the group while in fact they may be more focused on their own well-being, much like the animal counterpart.

Our workplace counterparts are similar in types of communications. They usually are motivated by short comments and conversations. They will limit their expression to need and or function in nature. Primarily they are looking for external threats to the group and that is what they will respond to most readily.

Tips for dealing with a Monitoring Meerkat behaviour

1. Understand this behaviour can seem like a nervous habit but it has at its core is a genuine concern for the group so

it does serve a positive role. While you may not see them as the strongest or the most dedicated member of the team they are comfortable in the role they have, so embrace it.

2. Keep in mind this behaviour can exhibit some selfish characteristics in that it will generally not challenge internal issues. It will flow with internal politics and, hopefully, keep a low profile, unless there is an external threat, so you cannot expect it to be internally active 100% of the time. It will provide an escalated level of activity based on the perceived threat to the group but remain engaged the rest of the time.

3. This behaviour may cause some to become so resolute in their stand for getting justice that they will become extremely active in pursuit of a specific resolution and lose site of the big picture. The key here is to help them to stay focused on the big picture and not become too distracted by a singular motivation.

4. This behaviour can also be transitional. It may not be a permanent part of a person's work effort because, like the animal counterparts, the role may shift between a number of people over a period of time. This may in fact be a very positive factor for the enterprise because you can grow people from this behaviour to extremely active and engaged leaders by using their social nature.

From an energetic Meerkat we jump to an equally energetic Tenacious Terrier. Terriers are typically agile and very driven to the point they appear hyperactive.

Tenacious Terrier

Agile, Driven

Terrier Description

The Tenacious Terrier is the archetypal dog with a bone. It is muscular and taut, and clever to the point of cunning, with exceptional agility and explosive attacking energy.

Imagine a nine-inch length of thick rope, knotted and frayed at both ends. A Terrier wrestles with it in his mouth, shaking it and chewing hard. The rope is the complex knotted weave of tasks and strategies, situations and priorities, challenges and opportunities that we all face in the world of work. The Tenacious Terrier has something of the wolf about it, as any dog does. Like wolves, dogs tend to hunt in packs, so the there is always potential for the Tenacious Terrier to be a good team worker. More commonly, however, the Tenacious Terrier is a bit of a lone wolf, for unlike foxhounds, Terriers are bred and used to hunt alone rather than in a pack. The single-handed (single pawed?) aspect of Tenacious Terrier behaviour is surpassed only by its single-mindedness.

Tenacious Terrier behaviour in the wild

A friend recently remarked that while on safari In Africa, she was quite comfortable driving and even walking near to lions, hyenas and rhinos, but when the wild hunting dogs appeared in the distance the sense of threat was palpable. It was immediately obvious that the dogs were planning their group strategy for attack. Even the safari leader got nervous, telling everyone to stay in the vehicle and wind their windows up tight.

The dog is not just the most vicious and feared animal out there though; three million pet owners in the UK alone show that it is also the most loyal and the most loved. This combination of fear and love connotes admiration and respect. In addition, if that goes for dogs, in general it goes for Terriers in particular, for they are the most intelligent and the most effective hunters of all dogs. If there is any Tenacious Terrier behaviour in your workplace, you definitely want it on your side, not working against you!

Tenacious Terrier behaviour in the workplace

Tenacious Terrier behaviour is highly adaptable; it can thrive in all environments, from the comfy casual vibe to the cut and thrust of even the most wild and hostile terrain. In any environment, this critter will emerge as top dog and will not stop battling until it does.

Tenacious Terrier behaviour is a relentless pursuit of solutions towards the speediest possible successful attainment of target requirements for any given objective.

Not all work objectives are fully attainable, some contexts and conditions are just too complex to balance out and some problems are wicked or insoluble. The Tenacious Terrier may not always succeed in unravelling and conquering that rope bone, but none could try harder or with greater purpose and determination. If the Terrier can't, no dog can!

If the Tenacious Terrier sniffs a goal, it will stop at nothing to achieve it. If challenged by colleagues, its alpha leader character emerges; and if challenged by competitors its bite is worse than its bark!

While Donkey behaviour is stubborn "I won't do x" with a negative motto of "I won't I won't I won't" Terrier behaviour is persistent "I will not stop until I have accomplished x", with a positive motto of" I will I will I will" – regardless of other people or other objectives.

Despite being exceptionally intelligent and loyal Terriers are not easily trained, but do not be put off by someone who exhibits Tenacious Terrier behaviour, they bring more good than bad. They make sure things get done. They are reluctant to change, and focused to the point of being one track minded. If you are managing someone with this behaviour, getting it right is a very rewarding challenge requiring strong and clear leadership.

This behaviour can resemble bullying, riding roughshod over the more delicate sensibilities of less the robust, such as for example the Minimal Mouse. Again, if you find this attitude, it is a case for firm handling. If, on the other hand, this behaviour comes from your boss there is no point brown-nosing; you had better get good at playing grab-ass if you want to have anything to sit down on at the end of the day.

Tips for harnessing Tenacious Terrier behaviour

If you encounter Tenacious Terrier behaviour in the workplace, how should you react?

1. Appealing to its creative and playful side is always worth a go; the adaptability and flexibility of this behaviour type combines with its boundless enthusiasm and dogged determination to make most desirable workplace behaviour.
2. No need to try to tame it, as it is fiercely loyal already and does not bite the hand that feeds it. Just allow it to be a positive influence, spreading energy, enthusiasm and a genuine can-do attitude.
3. Marvel at its twisting and turning, its bouncing and pouncing, its running and cunning, and be glad that it is on your side.
4. Use their tenacity to inspire drive in others.
5. Do not tease or antagonise the person exhibiting this kind of behaviour – its bite is worse than its bark! Do not 'brown-nose'. Play grab-ass or get chewed!

The Tenacious Terrier behaviour is playful but intense so now we go the playful in the form of the Cheeky Chimp who is both energetic and creative. Let's go find a Chimp, tongue in cheek, of course.

Cheeky Chimp

Energetic, Creative

Chimp Description

The Cheeky Chimp is a creative, curious and provocative disruptor, an improviser and a good learner. The character of Chimp behaviour is seen in the Ancient Oriental tale of The Monkey whose gung-ho adventurous nature is matched by his fearless integrity. The Cheeky Chimp is characterised by boundless energy, relentless persistence and the ability to do things, and to put ideas together, in unexpected ways. Play is how animals learn and the Chimp's play is evidence of their capacity for learning, which is further demonstrated in their unique ability to learn and adapt to new cultural codes on joining different social groups.

Don't be deluded by the caricature of Chimps as 'cheeky', this is an artificial human construct. We often perceive them to be cute, funny, slightly dim but creative versions of ourselves. This image is reinforced through children's books, films, and cuddly toys but it is not accurate. In fact, they are much more complex than that and a genus in their own right. Because of their high level of social and cultural sophistication, their young have much to learn and play is how adults teach them. Chimps are capable of violence, promiscuity, drunkenness and a whole gamut of human-like traits, which lead us to anthropomorphise them.

Chimp behaviour in the wild

Chimps are actually highly social animals, with clear hierarchic structures to their communities and work activities such as hunting. The Chimp shares 99% of our DNA, so it is the closest thing to human. It is physically robust (what they lack in intelligence they make up for in brute strength compared to us) and extremely agile with a particularly good sense of balance. It is almost as if they have four hands, which help them swing through the even densest jungle with ease. They are adventurous explorers and intelligent experimenters, fashioning rudimentary tools such as sticks for harvesting ants and macerating leaves to make sponges. They also seem to display a sense of humour, along with a capacity for manipulation and deception, which is most unusual in the animal world. Finally, the Chimp has a notably sophisticated range of communication skills including vocalisation, gesturing and even laughter.

Chimp behaviour in the workplace

Cheeky Chimp behaviour reminds us of Levi Strauss' anthropological distinction between the bricoleur type of thinking and the engineer. While the engineer mind-set is systematic and linear, the bricoleur seems almost chaotic by comparison, with more improvisation and thinking outside the box. While the engineer follows a narrow but tightly focused thought and development process, the bricoleur stumbles on discovery and innovation through an attitude of playful curiosity.

The sometimes apparently randomly spread creative energy combines with a matchless persistence to make Cheeky Chimp behaviour a creative wellspring of innovation. Their playful capacity for learning also marks the Chimp as highly trainable; it is a wise manager who invests in training people exhibiting such traits.

The Cheeky Chimp is a great disruptor. This is not just to say they make a mess of any system or tea party. Disruption in the context of innovation means much more than that; it signifies the ability to use out of the box thinking to develop new ideas, which render obsolete existing models, processes and systems. E.g. electricity (disrupted oil, gas and steam energy) electric light bulb (disrupted use of daytime only working), personal computers (disrupted typewriters and manual filing), smart phones (disrupted where your workplace is), discount retailers (disrupted fixed pricing), the Internet (disrupted localism), Social Media (disrupted the need for physical contact), Skype (disrupted telephony), credit card (disrupted the cash economy).

This innovative flair can make Cheeky Chimp behaviour unpopular at times, especially in a more conservative work culture. Cheeky Chimp behaviour can seem socially unskilled too, but it is worth remembering that Chimps are actually very social animals, and this kind of behaviour in the workplace is usually well intended; their disruption is seldom malicious, just playful. This innocence is why Chimps are often seen as cute. Its youthful aspect also plays a part here; their lively behaviour will liven up any room they come into.

The adventurous and curious aspect of Cheeky Chimp behaviour is great for processes of discovery, but it can also open Pandora's Box. Not that this worries them, for when the woes are released our Chimp will play with them with no other protection than fearless innocence. Groups of Chimps can make this curiosity factor more accentuated, complex and difficult to manage, but the potential for breakthroughs is higher too – remember the Shakespeare experiment. [4]

Another key point about Cheeky Chimp behaviour is its emotional load. Chimps are emotionally expressive across

---

[4] The Shakespeare experiment theorised "that a monkey hitting keys at random on a typewriter keyboard for an infinite amount of time will almost surely type a given text, such as the complete works of William Shakespeare." (Wikipedia)

the whole spectrum from excitement, love, and joy to frustration, sorrow and aggression. They feel things deeply. Their tendency not to filter means that you know what is on their mind, and where you stand with them at any given moment. You always know what they are feeling, which can be an advantage or not depending how you choose to frame it.

It is also worth bearing in mind that because of their sensitivity and spontaneity their behaviour can switch quickly and unexpectedly. As long as it is not riled or over-stressed, Cheeky Chimp behaviour adds value to any work-team and you should welcome it - in its place.

Tips for engaging with Cheeky Chimp behaviour

1. Invest in training to channel creativity and innovation. They will appreciate it and make good use of it.
2. Give them knotty problems and see the innovative solutions they find. They are supreme problem solvers.
3. They are more suited to discovery than analytic tasks. Not for them are the mundane administration activities that others will be much better at.
4. Look for the positive value of any disruption caused. Disruption is not always a bad thing.
5. Use them in leadership roles where cultural change is indicated. Not all leaders can cope with an uncertain environment. Chimps do.

6. Do not try to harness their creativity but give it free reign to realise its full value. Consult and use where creative thinking is required.

Cheeky Chimps are very social and very active. However, the next animal the Fawning Feline is usually isolated and standoffish in their environment. Not the purrfect match in some environments.

Fawning Feline

Obsequious, Self-Centred

The door opens and a small sleek shape slips into the room. Miaow, cries a plaintive voice, as a huge pair of glistening eyes turn imploringly towards you. Miaow! The eyes grow even larger and you think 'so cute!' and your hand reaches down unconsciously to stroke a soft sleek head. Miaow! Your legs work automatically to transport you to the kitchen where, with practised ease, you open a pouch of food and place it in the small bowl on the floor. Prrr, prrr, prrr you hear as a soft body bumps your leg on its way to the full bowl. The food disappears quickly and your Feline is gone as quickly as it arrived.

Description of the domestic Fawning Feline

Physically, Felines are renowned for their flexibility and ability to survive even quite large falls. They are able to twist and turn until they land safely on their feet. This extraordinary ability for survival has led to the widely held belief that they have 'nine lives'.

Felines, like their larger relatives, are carnivores. Like most carnivores, they are programmed to spend a large part of their day asleep. Most will continue to hunt and kill small prey, if given the opportunity. They are active both day and night, with a preference for night hunting. Being quite adaptable, domesticated Felines will vary their routine to suit the humans amongst whom they live. Once they establish their routine however, they do like to stick to it for as long as possible. Habits die hard with a domestic cat.

Felines appear widely in mythology, from being revered as gods and goddesses to being burnt alive as bad luck symbols and witches familiars; where they cause fear simply by association. They are sometimes associated with good luck, and sometimes bad. It seems humans have always been fascinated by the very mystery and unpredictability of Feline behaviour.

Feline behaviour in the wild

History suggests that Felines began domesticating humans over 8000 years ago, possibly even longer. They are now the most popular 'pet' in the world and reside in almost every place where humans live. Despite their reputation for being 'loners', they are a social species with a wide range of vocalisations and body language, which they use to great effect with their human hosts. Unlike domestic dogs, domestic Felines have retained a high degree of independence, and frequently breed with feral Feline populations. Unlike dogs, they are rarely subjected to 'training', although they are equally intelligent and fond of playing.

There is a great deal of information written about the behaviour of Felines, such is our fascination with them. There are many books written about how to interpret their body language, posture, sounds, food preferences, and endless videos of Felines doing unusual things such as sitting on an automated vacuum cleaner wearing a shark suit (really!) Because of their apparent integration into our lives, we express great interest in the nuances of their behaviour. Yet, we do not truly understand them.

Essentially, Felines are past masters at adapting their behaviour to whatever is required to fulfil their own goals. This can make them appear to be unpredictable and yet predictable at the same time they are creatures of adaptable habit.

Identifying Feline behaviour in the workplace

Workplace Fawning Feline behaviour is generally very popular. They express charisma and easiness to be around. Even though this, fawning behaviour can be obvious, Felines do it with such finesse and charm, that they get away with it! This should be annoying, but Felines do it with such ease and apparent artlessness, that the recipient cannot help but feel better for it.

Although quite flexible in some ways, being creatures of routine they do not like change particularly. Their flexibility is mainly focussed on persuading other people to help them gain something they really want or in getting them out of trouble.

They are often too busy being charming to be particularly ambitious, but they are quite territorial. More than almost anyone else, they really understand workplace politics.

In extremes, this Fawning Feline behaviour can become an irritant and a distraction to getting work done. This excess of irrelevant and empty words can keep attention away from discussing important issues. At their worst, this charm can smooth a path to a more senior position than other skills deserve, or whispered beads of poison drip into the ears of a naïve boss can create the illusion of calm or success where this does not exist.

Although you will find Felines fawning anywhere and everywhere, they are most common in places where there are many people to be charmed. Bureaucracy is a natural backdrop, as this provides the unchanging environment most conducive to this behaviour.

They rarely reach great heights in the management hierarchy, much to their regret, as they would really like a high position from which to survey the landscape. However, they rarely have the drive necessary for such positions. One possible exception to this is sales, in which they excel. This natural charm is particularly suited to persuading customers to buy almost anything.

Although they may appear to be thick skinned, they are not. They are likely to fight back when cornered, and have the claws and teeth to be quite effective. Never forget that, despite the charm, they are at heart, predators.

Tips for engaging with Fawning Feline behaviour

1. Charm requires a sensitivity to other people's feeling and motives, which works for both positive and negative responses. If they detect negativity from you, especially if they interpret it as personal, you are likely to receive a substantial fight back. They have the claws and teeth to be quite effective, both literally and figuratively. Never forget that, despite the charm, they are at heart, predators.
2. Felines really understand and are in their element with workplace politics, whether they be in a physical or virtual workplace. On the one hand, they can be invaluable in helping you understand the nuances, on the other, they are unlikely to express a great deal of loyalty, so will always act in their best interest. Watch your back. However, provided you are aware of this, and give them

sufficient incentive to be on your side, they can be an invaluable aid in navigating the rapids of workplace politics.

3. The finesse of a Fawning Feline makes them supreme people, people. Harnessed by an effective incentive, they can be supreme negotiators.

4. Felines are vain and need frequent praise and 'stroking'. They respond very well to this as they truly live to be liked.

5. Fawning Felines do not handle change well, so will need additional support.

The Fawning Feline really understands the workplace politics that requires handling with kid gloves however; our next animal would rather run than fight. Off to the Ostentatious Ostrich.

Ostentatious Ostrich

Bluff, Showy

As we continue through the office jungle, we next observe the Ostentatious Ostrich behaviour. From a distance, you will see them clustered together throughout the workplace environment. Some are just standing around talking with an eye on the surrounding area to ensure a boss stopping by unexpectedly does not surprise them. You will find them congregating in small groups and there will usually be a dominant leader amongst the group.

Description of an Ostrich

Ostriches are a unique flightless bird that is built for running. It is a powerful bird reaching almost 400 pounds in the wild but it does come in all sizes. They have a life expectancy of 40 – 50 years today but they almost went extinct in the 1700 and 1800's due to extensive hunting for the feathers, which were prized for fashionistas of the day.

They are the fastest bird species, with a maximum running speed of more than 40 mph (64 kph), and they can cover 10 to 16 feet (3 to 5 meters) in a single stride. Ostriches can maintain a speed of 30 mph (48 kph) for long periods, helping them escape nearly any predator.

One of our authors commented, "Having visited the San Diego Zoo many times, I had become 'friends' with a male Ostrich in the compound; I called him 'Walt'. He was a majestic bird standing about six foot tall and easily supporting 275 pounds. After my second visit in a relatively short period, I noticed that he would begin to dance and prance when he saw me coming down the walkway."

This occurred every time he returned, even years later and yes; it was unique to him for some reason. "The head would bob and weave in anticipation that 'Walt' may want to engage me in a battle. Of course it was all show, indicated by the fact that when I got closer he would take off in a dead run for the other side of the compound." These motions are unique to the Ostrich and make them easy to spot.

Given its size and posturing, the Ostrich can convey a very aggressive position but it is usually a diversion. Its real goal is to use the power of its legs to burst speeds up to 40 mph or with a maintained speed of 30mph to avoid a predator.

They are protective of their young with both the male and female playing a role.

Ostrich behaviour in the wild

The Ostrich is normally found in arid regions of the world including Africa and Arab countries. However due to the expansion of Ostrich ranching to raise them for feathers, leather and meat they have a presence in many countries worldwide. The Ostrich has a very large set of eyes, up to 2" in diameter, set upon a very long neck and they are very observant of their surroundings.

As has been mentioned, the Ostrich is normally a non-fighter even though they can exhibit a bit of aggressive behaviour at times. The sway of the long neck and the movement of its large three toed feet, both of which can inflict damage to anyone who chooses to attack, usually indicate this. The neck for example has been known to break a predator's spine in one swing. In reality though, this dance and prance is usually a diversion so the rest of the flock can flee.

The best-known visual of an Ostrich is the perceived burying of the head in the sand. This however is a myth that is typically driven by the action it takes when a predator threatens its nest. An Ostrich will flop to the ground and remain, laying its head against the sand to try to blend in with it. Only its body is visible, so from a distance, it looks like the Ostrich has buried its head in the sand.

On a side note, it is interesting that in 2012 a design group from Europe; Kawamura & Ganjavian came up with the Ostrich Pillow. The whole concept is based on the theory that a power nap will allow a person to be up to 34% more productive so the pillow provides the environment that is soft, comfortable and dark. I can imagine people pulling on their Ostrich pillows and sleeping at their desks now, yeah right. This could be the next response of an ostentatious office Ostrich if things become tough.

Ostrich behaviour in the workplace

You can usually identify Ostentatious Ostrich behaviour by an attention to preening, and the style with which it carries it out. Like their counterparts in the wild, this attitude exhibits a concern with putting on a show if someone is watching. If there is nothing around that threatens them or intimidates them, they are usually just going about the day-to-day grind.

Likewise, in the work environment the Ostrich is usually found where the environment is very predictable and comfortable. It does not like having to bolt around frantically even though they are very unpredictable themselves. Similarly, in our office jungle the Ostrich behaviour is very similar, in that it is constantly scanning the immediate area for something they feel they need to react to by either fight or flight.

In the office, this type of behaviour is usually seen in terms of a show that may be construed as a confrontation using big words and fancy arguments to divert attention away from actual resolution of a problem or successful completion of a project. This allows the other Ostrich behaving people to run and hide. They would much rather avoid a confrontation than stay and face it.

In the office, we can see the Ostrich having an influence on younger workers who might be looking for some protection. Ostriches may also be looking for the supervisor showing up unexpectedly, thereby requiring them to take to a run. They will typically avoid confrontation, until they are backed into a corner. Then they can become quite aggressive.

Tips for dealing with Ostrich behaviour

1. When this behaviour appears in a boss or supervisor you need to be very aware of how the behaviour affects others. It has a tendency for making other tense and somewhat skittish in the presence of the senior leader.
2. If you are managing one or more people who exhibit Ostrich behaviour, then you need to allow them to feel secure and unthreatened so they can be productive. Note that they live on a constant alert basis so it is critical to remove potential unpredictable activities from occurring.
3. If you feel you are exhibiting this behaviour, then it is important to look at why you are so driven by the fight or flight actions. Learn skills that help you control the impulses, so you can control it for the good of the team or group.
4. Be aware that regardless of where this behaviour appears, there is a preference to avoid confrontation and

run from any threat. It is very possible that people with this behaviour will spend a lot of time performing yet not really producing anything of a positive nature. However, an excellent team environment calls for active participation from all members without exception so the source of threat must be minimised for a person with this behaviour to participate well.

The Ostrich puts on a good show but it usually prefer to run than fight. Our next animal, the Giant Clam, never goes anywhere so they are usually secretive and unyielding.

Giant Clam

Secretive, Unyielding

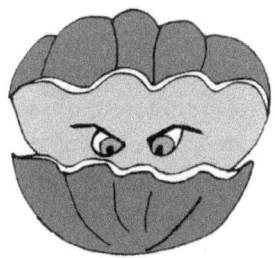

Do you have someone in your workplace who seems to have been there for a long time with no interest of going anywhere else in the company? That person is very reminiscent of the next animal in our jungle, the Giant Clam.

Many times this person has survived through multiple leaders, and possible various mergers or acquisitions, hopefully with a positive attitude, even though they choose not to move anywhere. Like the Giant Clam, they feel that they have only one chance to find a nice home and the make a series of symbiotic agreements with other forms of life to grow and flourish.

Description of a Giant Clam

The Giant Clam will drift until it can find a home where there is sufficient food, atmosphere and light that it can live its 100 or more years of life. Generally, it is at the mercy of the currents so the level of choice is slim to say the least but there is a choice none the less. They can grow to be 440 pounds in weight and have girth of 4 feet being fed by the sugars and proteins produced by the billions of algae that live in their tissues. In return, they provide a home and regular access to sunlight for photosynthesis as they bask below the surface of the water with their shells open and their mantles exposed. They also use a siphon to draw in water so they can filter water and consume the passing plankton. They hold a position of respect in the underwater society with few enemies with man being the predominant predator.

Giant Clam in the wild

The Giant Clam has an extremely undeserved reputation as a man-eater with a number of legends arising out of South Pacific 'lore'. These stories seem to indicate that the Clam will clamp down on an unsuspecting persons foot as they swim by and then consume them. However, the abductor muscle, which closes the shell, is excessively slow to catch a human by surprise. With this excuse out of the way, man will consume the abductor muscle because it is considered a delicacy and the shell is often taken as a trophy so man is the aggressor.

Giant Clam behaviour in the workplace

After reviewing this animal, we can jump back to the correlation between the Giant Clam and a human worker exhibits some of the same characteristics in some situations.

Similar to the Giant Clam, we can see that this behaviour can be beneficial to the organisation due to the depth of knowledge and time in the trenches. Yes, the person with this attitude has been in one job or series of jobs for a long time, and yes, they have no desire to change or move to a different department. Many enterprises today view this behaviour as a negative factor. The person's job may seem to be low hanging fruit for cost savings and employee reductions but there should be a careful examination made before this decision is finalised. Their loyalty and knowledge may be more valuable if used to expand new members of the team and to grow them similar to how a Giant Clam provides a home to the algae to flourish.

While the average employee with this attitude will not make useful contributions for 100 years like the Giant Clam, there are many circumstances where the person can provide value and support for a longer period of time than the normal duration on a job, reflective of other people today, who may change job or career every 5 years.

Be wise in your approach with this person. Understand their needs and desires and weigh the costs of replacement carefully because like a Giant Clam they are beautiful at what they do and may be worth nurturing. Many times their reputation is legendary in terms of how they have stayed in their position for so long so do not let them suffer from a similar undeserved reputation, like the Giant Clam.

Tips for dealing with Giant Clam behaviour

1. If you work for a boss that has this behaviour you must be very careful in how you submit new ideas and program changes to them. Make sure you have all of their questions anticipated before you start explaining the idea.

2. When you manage this type of person, take time to understand what makes them tick. What do they have a handle on that others are struggling with and how can you leverage their knowledge. Do not make them a target of reduction unless you have an effective plan for backfilling their knowledge. Remember they can be very established in the environment and the may be critical the overall operations of the department or company.

3. If you have this behaviour pattern and know that you are in fact working in this pattern, you need to understand your position in the company. Understand how you bring value to the team and ensure that you reinforce this on a regular basis. Take time to expand your skill sets and expand your internal outreach to ensure your own growth.

4. Regardless of the location of this behaviour, you should note that the one affected could develop an attitude of entitlement that must be guarded against. Once this line has been crossed, the effectiveness of the behaviour will be reduced significantly because there is no perceived flexibility within the team or group. In today's market that is a dangerous position to be in at any point.

5. Never take Giant Clam behaviour personally; even if they tell you it is, personal it is not. Others may think of it as a bad attitude to have but in reality, this behaviour may

have a solid foot in reality that needs to be preserved. Think of this behaviour as anchoring behaviour, it comes from a part of the mind that is somewhat linked to the past but it can be flexible.

The Giant Clam can be secretive and unyielding in some environments yet they may be really feeling entitled. The key is it might be good or bad. The next animal behaviour we need to approach with caution. The Prickly Porcupine can be a bit thorny to work with.

Prickly Porcupine

Petulant, Unreceptive

As you are walking down a country road or sitting at a campground you may see the relatively large lumbering animal meandering around, it is grey to black with white accents that seems to be slicked back into a furdoo. In reality, it is a Prickly Porcupine and we will see how you can identify this creature in the work place.

Description of a Porcupine

Porcupines are the second largest rodent in North America. They weigh between 11 and 30 pounds, and are 23 to 48 inches long. Porcupines have a stocky, slow, lumbering form and a spiny coat. They usually appear dark brown to black, although some of the hairs and quills on the backs of these animals are yellow.

Porcupines have quills on their backs from the head to the tail. Many of their quills are outlined with white, which makes them stand out against the dark fur underneath. Quills are usually 3 - 4 inches long. Each quill has microscopic barbs on the tip which assists them stick into a Porcupine's enemies. The quills are not hollow, but are filled with a spongy matrix, which makes them very rigid and light. Each Porcupine has approximately 30,000 quills. Once these quills embed themselves, they are designed to move deeper into a predator, encouraging them to move away for fear of further impalement.

All Porcupines have long claws. These claws help them climb on both large tree trunks and surprisingly small branches. The palms and soles of Porcupines have a pebbly surface and no fur. Along with their keen sense of touch, this special texture on the hands and feet improves a Porcupine's grip. Because they are so good at gripping trees, Porcupines can even stay in trees using only their hind feet to hold on. This frees their forelimbs for use in eating.

Porcupine behaviour in the wild

Porcupines have a tendency to be nocturnal in travel and foraging but they will venture out in the day if necessary; they are not migratory and will inhabit a relatively small geographic footprint. They do not hibernate during the winter but will limit the amount of activity to conserve energy and nutrition.

Socially, they are loners; however, they will share a den when necessary for protection from the elements. This is contrary to many herbivores that are more communal. Availability of den space in the area, drives their den sharing, i.e. fewer dens, more sharing.

Porcupines will communicate acoustically, chemically and visually in nature. When approached they would prefer to run up a tree rather than confront but if necessary they will provide an audible discourse, teeth gnashing and become physically agitated. There is misinformation regarding the quills. Many will say that a Porcupine throws its quills at the predator but this is not true.

Porcupines use their quills in two ways. Quills actually form a shield made of barbed quills. They can also drive the quills into the predator. Once a Porcupine has stuck its quills into an enemy, the Porcupine needs to quickly separate from the quills. To do this, these animals have evolved unique quill-release systems. Erect quills release easier from the Porcupine after they push them into the would-be predator's body.

Porcupine behaviour in the workplace

Prickly Porcupine behaviour is easy to spot. People with this tendency will appear to be unsocial and have a tendency to come in late and work late. They will not migrate very far from their assigned work area unless asked to do so and they will be uncomfortable in that role. They will be diligent workers when left alone.

Territorial behaviour is common. Therefore, our workplace Porcupine will knows its territory quite well and usually does not venture too far from it; the main exceptions are excursions to get the equivalent of the Porcupine's salt or apples.

Generally, people will respect those with Porcupine tendencies, but will have limited engagement due to a fear of receiving the quills by being too close. Although workplace Porcupine quills are not physical but verbal or emotional, they carry a similar sting and are equally difficult to remove.

This solitary preference does not attract many fans or co-workers within his assigned work area. Even when part of a team, he prefers accountability to be for only his or her work not the team output.

Ambition is not a primary driver and they do not really understand workplace politics. To them, you do your job as best you can and try to enjoy the experience. Lack of ambition also means no particular desire for promotion either, so they are unlikely to push to participate outside of their assigned work to gain more visibility. They would much more prefer to remain in their own territory for their life span at the company.

If pushed, like their wildlife brethren, you will see them use their version of the quills as a shield. If pushed further, they will turn around and seek to embed the quills deep into the perceived predator.

You will find Prickly Porcupines almost anywhere, but they are most comfortable in places where the environment protects them from the predators of the workplace. Like in the wild, where they are herbivores, the workplace Porcupine will not act in aggressive manner until threatened. However, if there is the equivalent of salt in the workplace the Porcupine will go outside of its territory.

Their slow moving and methodical approach to tasks can result in their competence not being widely recognised.

However, in a world where people can become easily isolated, they have an important role to play. One of the challenges of remote working and ecollaboration is the need to build closer connections and trust. If there is much work that can be done independently then a Porcupine with the necessary skills can be an asset since it will only need to socialise when asked to do so.

This desire for solitariness may lead you to believe that they are thick skinned - they are not. They are really quite sensitive on the underside and from the front and are quite vigilant in watching for a negative approach. If you are able to keep the quills in check, they can be quite productive.

Porcupines don't do intimacy. They will not willingly share their personal information beyond what is strictly necessary, and rarely make friends at work. For them, home is home, work is work.

In summary, the workplace Porcupine will be productive as long as they are comfortable with the territory. They do have the potential to let the quills loose when challenged so you must be aware of this when dealing with them.

Tips for engaging with Prickly Porcupine behaviour

1. Take advantage of their ability to work alone. Not all work requires the ability to work in a team interactively.
2. Give them the detailed work that others find boring, but where their diligence and methodical approach can be really useful e.g. financial figure work, software code development or testing etc.
3. Give them a safe place to work from where they are not subjected to regular interference by other people. They can be safely trusted to work from home, although you should have an agreed timetable for contact. Without this, they will not call back into the workplace.
4. No sudden moves! Change makes them nervous and liable to respond with a verbal barb or negative action. When you need to make changes, make sure you plan communications with plenty of time to assimilate the details. Do not expect an instant response – not a positive one anyway!
5. If you want them to get involved with thinking creatively, do not invite them to an interactive workshop, which they will hate, but ask them to contribute their ideas via a suggestion scheme instead.

The Prickly Porcupine behaviour can a bit difficult to work with in a group; it can be found working alone very well.

Next, we meet another loner, the Angry Alligator. Much more dangerous, he may look slow but watch out for his rapid lunge.

Angry Alligator

Rude, Intimidating

Alligator Description

The Angry Alligator is a bit of a dinosaur. This fearsome tyrant represents a primitive aspect of animal behaviour, which can be described as 'reptilian'. Its style of predation is crude but effective. They might not look like it but they can sprint short distances up to 30 mph! Alligators have the patience of the ancients sometimes waiting days for a suitable kill; with lightening quick reactions, when they strike it is explosive and decisive, totally without warning. Despite being somewhat lumbering and resistant to change, their thickly armoured skin and sheer muscular bulk help to make them the consummate survivor.

Alligator behaviour in the wild

Inhabiting watering holes and swamplands, the Alligator is a stealthy predator, often submerged or hidden in the reeds. They live in social groups but they are anything but hospitable. Every Alligator is a loner deep down with little or no sense of loyalty or responsibility for the group. The exception to this is their mothering, which is fiercely protective and surprisingly soft. It may have a lethal bite and no bark, but when you see an Alligator carrying its own egg in those fearsome teeth you realise they are quite capable of being gentle and nurturing when they want to be. Aside from this, they live in the groups and habitats they find themselves in but they do not really do 'friends' as such.

Sadly, damage to their environment threatens the extinction of Alligators in the wild, but the behaviour of these reptilian throwbacks still proliferates in the workplace. Would that it were the other way round!

Angry Alligator behaviour in the workplace

Angry Alligator behaviour is high on giving information, proposing, disagreeing and shutting out. It often deals with other people and their ideas by refusing to listen and cutting them short, and then goes on to explain why the first speaker was wrong. In arguments, it tends to use many 'irritators' and often descends into defend / attack: "You are not listening to me - I'll tell you again."

If you find one in the room during a meeting or team task, a one to one conversation will often get to the root of the problem, which may well involve external 'baggage' (they had a bad day or whatever). We are talking about the behaviour of an animal that stopped adapting when it found its unique niche in the ecosystem, and with adaptation being so low on its list of qualities they can be slow to get over something that troubled them some time before.

Alligator behaviour is typically angry when contradicted. It's almost as if the person behaving like this does not understand the world they're in, the social world of dialogue, of give and take within groups and teams where ideas are often challenged in order to be refined. Alligators don't do 'dialogue' or 'refined'.

Because of this thick-skinned solitary aspect, Angry Alligator behaviour can seem impermeable to reason and change; acting and thinking like an Alligator is not ideal for learning, hence it can seem relatively simplistic and un-evolved, relying on stealth and brute strength.

In general, Alligator behaviour tends to be more solitary than social and can appear to be quite self-contained. It seems almost oblivious to others as long as they keep a safe distance, but woe betides the colleague who strays into their territory.

All this behaviour reflects a general limitedness in communication skills. Communication with someone in Alligator mode tends to be one way, they don't listen well.

Training can help here, but will only be effective if it addresses the reptilian mind-set at the root of this behaviour.

The fact that they tend to inhabit swamps reflects the point that Angry Alligator behaviours thrive most in workplace environments that are operating on infirm and boggy ground where systems are unwieldy, where progress of the narrative of the organisation is slow, improvement of working conditions is sticky and CPD[5] is restricted and heavy going.

One final word of advice: Alligators have even been known to eat each other when there's no softer butt to chew on, in the workplace and in the wild alike. Don't take it personally if they chew on yours.

Tips for staying safe around Angry Alligator behaviour

1. If your boss is an Angry Alligator, tread lightly and look for a way out. The whole company is likely to become mired in the negativity of its cold-blooded reptilian ethos.
2. If you manage an Angry Alligator, try to use their unshakable single mindedness by giving them tasks where it is a benefit. If you need someone to do or announce something unpopular here is your ideal choice:

---

[5] CPD - Continuing professional development

nobody will want to confront them and their thick skin makes them more or less indifferent to critical whispers.

3. If you have to work as an equal with an Angry Alligator, be sure you are clear about your territory and stick to it. As long as you keep your distance, you will be safe. They only charge if their space is threatened.

4. If you find yourself acting out like an Angry Alligator, it is important to make human connection ASAP. Confide in someone about the behaviour. Change may be slow but it is a start.

5. Never take Angry Alligator behaviour personally, even if they tell you it is personal - it isn't. They cannot be really personal because there is too much pre-human about their behaviour. Think of this behaviour as 'pre-personal', it comes from a part of the mind that is reptilian.

Even the Angry Alligator can provide some positive influence in the workspace but our next animal is one that has little good to report. They are often compared to a bloodsucker and most times, they live up to the comparison. Welcome the Lasting Leech to the group. Suck it up and let's discuss.

Lasting Leech

Bloodsucking, Selfish

Leech Description

The Leech is really a segmented worm based on normal biological classification. The reason we have included it in our list is more from a perception of their role in life than reality for the most part. We have a paranoia about them when it comes to swimming or wandering in wet lands.

Leeches look like large earthworms, but are perceived as much more terrifying to handle and tolerate because most people do not understand them. They have a segmented body that is very flexible. Their equivalent of a brain spreads across the various segments, which is unique. They can range in colour from black to red with variations occurring over the spectrum. There are some 700 different species recognised by biologist today. Usually they are very distinctive and highly recognisable after walking in a stream or bog.

Most Leeches live in freshwater; however, there are some that are terrestrial or found in saltwater. Most are quite literally bloodsuckers feasting on vertebrate and invertebrate animals that are readily available in their locations and thankfully, the majority do not necessarily focus on human blood due to an abundant supply of smaller species. In fact, many will rely on decomposing bodies and open wounds of available amphibians.

They have been used as medicinal tools, appearing in ancient Greece and India extending well into the 19th century as a practice. In modern times, the medicinal practice can still be found especially in the areas of reattachment of limbs and skin grafts.

Leech behaviour in the wild

Most Leeches use body waving or head motion to attract potential hosts but they will take advantage of any target that comes within their area of purview. In this way, they are an opportunist. They can also utilise the flow of the water to ride and find a new location for finding good host materials.

The biggest influences a Leech has in the fear created by the sight of them attached to a host. The perception is that they are dangerous and some even feel it may be able to drain a host however; they will usually disconnect themselves when they become full which is usually between 20 minutes and 2 hours of attachment. To remove it is usually recommended that you use a finger or blunt object to break the suction.

Most experts do not recommend using heat or other technique to remove a Leech because it may force them to detach and vomit stomach contents onto the wound and this can be dangerous.

We call it a Lasting Leech because of the difficulty of removing them if they attach themselves to one's body. Because of the varieties in the environment one must be patient in removing them to avoid any complications but they are not as dangerous as many people feel they are.

Workplace Leech behaviour

A Leech behaviour driven co-worker may refer to an attitude that continually wants more from us no matter how much we give them. It will usually refuse to reciprocate our efforts in any meaningful ways.

Leeching opportunists are diverse and endless. A co-worker constantly asks us to engage in useless conversation and is incensed when we decline. Another co-worker can routinely ask us to perform favours or lend him tools, yet never offers to lend us a hand when necessary. A co-worker is always happy to join us for happy hour, but disappears when it is his turn to pick up the tab. This behaviour can take on many different reflections.

Whatever the situation, the result is usually the same. Energy in the relationship travels one way. Recipients of leeching feel frustrated and drained. We may feel they are being taken for a ride. We long to stop the drain on their time, emotions and finances. Often we are frequently at a loss about how to divert or stop the flow.

Many times this leeching creates a subtle stress that is often un-recognised until it is out of control. Often the recipients report feeling guilty saying no to a Leeches demands. We dread hurting the chronic takers feelings. We worry about damaging the relationship.

In truth, the Leech attitude does not respect us anyway. Any relationship is distorted at best. They only want what they can get from us. When the supply runs out, they will happily move on to someone else.

Generally, as good co-workers, we are eager to help each other so when leeching takes place the connection and dialogue between individuals will begin to deteriorate and disappear. If this process takes place over a long period then resentment and possible damaging emotions may begin to appear. It is a one sided process without exception.

If the situation occurs between two co-workers that are not peers there may be some extenuating circumstances that need to be dealt with in the relationship. For example, it may be impossible for the weaker person to reciprocate for various reasons. If this is truly the case then the more endowed participant must determine their own intent and look at the relationship from a more compassionate point of view. This is where Emotional Intelligence comes to play in the arrangement.

The key to surviving this type of relationship is to understand that a Leech does not have good control over their interpretation of boundaries. They are by nature opportunist, they either do not understand protocol or they do not care. They will continue to take advantage of a situation as long as the host is willing to give.

This is where choice comes to play. A Leech must have willing hosts who are willing to continue to feed their needs. They scan the environment and look for willing participants to whom they can attach themselves and refuse to let go.

While there are similarities between a true Leech and a workplace Leech attitude, the focus should be the same in either case. The goal is to remove the Leech behaviour from the situation so that neither is damaged permanently. While a normal Leech may disconnect itself automatically after it has been satisfied the Workplace Leech behaviour needs to be helped to determine where the boundary is and disconnect.

Tips for surviving a Lasting Leech

Recognise leeching behaviour. Do they seem to always make demands on your money or time? Do they seem unappreciative about what you do? Do you have trouble setting limits on your relationship?

1. When dealing with peer-to-peer situation when one has the Leech behaviour attitude: understand and handle the guilt. When you worry that your negative response will

damage the relationship, focus on understanding your fears. How realistic is, the fear and what would be the worst that would happen if you said "NO". Remember, you are doing the right thing, protecting your boundaries while teaching your Leech an invaluable lesson.

2. When dealing with a boss or supervisor that exhibits this attitude, determine how to avoid over giving. Many workplace co-workers who exhibit Leech behaviour attach to people who make giving a way of life i.e., givers. Do not over-extend yourself in these situations. Give only what you comfortably can. Save ample emotional and physical resources for yourself and others who appreciate what you do.

3. Establish your personal boundaries. Lasting Leeches may want you to feel pressured so you will respond positively to the requests. Know when to back away. Respond to immediate requests by responding with a "Let me think about it". Then, go home and analyse what you really want to do. Use a modified SWOT analysis to find how you can embrace or whether you should disconnect. Remember, it is your career and you are in charge.

4. Institute a responsive methodology. You should use this if you are having trouble setting limits with others.

5. When asked to do something you do not feel comfortable doing, state two positive statements (i.e. "Thanks for thinking of me" and "You know I would love to help"), followed by your limit (But I am not able to fit this into my schedule at this time.) and one more positive statement (Hope you are able to accomplish your goal!).

Campfire Conversation

Have you found this useful?

We wrote this with the intent of it being a dynamic process, having fun and seeing our workplace in a new way. While each of our animal personas is whimsical, there are many ideas that will help you to build better working relationships, through observation of the various animal behaviours, adaptation and application of the Tips.

We hope you have enjoyed reading and learning about the Workplace Jungle as much as we enjoyed writing about it!

If you would like to continue the conversation, please go to our Facebook page:

https://www.facebook.com/groups/workplacejungle.2015/

About the Authors

Dr David Avery

As a culture dynamics consultant, David is passionate about using the stories that live in and around us to add meaning and value to human interaction and learning.

In his 20s, David moved from a successful sales background to study philosophy, anthropology, linguistics and mythology, and then spent several years teaching English and humanities in high schools and working as a university lecturer in education and culture dynamics.

In 2006, he founded the creative learning consultancy, Abracadia, providing workshops, training, coaching and mentoring for teachers and students to address behaviour management, engagement and culture-dynamics in schools. This led to David becoming a popular speaker at international conferences, taking on advisory roles with several local government bodies and writing for IPPR, a leading UK think tank.

In 2013, David expanded into the business world, founding Stories To Value (STV). STV uses creative thinking tools (data management frameworks, high resolution problem-solving games and 4D virtual reality computer programmes) developed from his Doctoral research to help companies reframe, reassess and improve productivity, manage change and information effectively and achieve sustainable growth by aligning the needs and perspectives of management, workers, markets and investors.

David also performs professionally as a jazz musician and a storyteller.

More at www.storiestovalue.com

Jacqui Hogan

 As a Management and Leadership specialist, Jacqui Hogan has been mentoring business owners, managers and directors to achieve their business goals since 2003. The combination of her technical IT background, empathy, people skills and systematic approach has delivered startling results for her clients.

Jacqui has wide experience in mentoring senior management and middle managers to be more effective. This includes both internal management responsibility, as well as practical experience managing difficult and challenging external client teams as an outsourced manager. Her experience is particularly strong in improving productivity, team building and developing managers within innovative IT companies, including those looking to improve their ecollaboration.

She has expertise in strategic planning and project management to deliver successful business solutions involving new ideas. She is particularly skilled in situations with a high degree of uncertainty or change: mentoring and motivating those involved and communicating effectively with stakeholders.

Jacqui is an experienced professional speaker on a wide range of management and non-management topics. She is also a regular blogger and you can share her management insights at http://www.cocreative.co.uk and on twitter @CoCreative. As an author, she wrote the popular management book '7 Things Remarkable Managers Do', now available on Amazon.

You can also find her on LinkedIn at http://www.linkedin.com/in/jacquihogan

Ron McIntyre

Proactive executive coach, Ron McIntyre is one of the co- authors of 'Together Works: The Ultimate Guide to Effective Ecollaboration'. He works with business owners, leaders in many different organisations that need change in their style of leadership, establishing their credibility, enhancing their reputation, positioning them to create a highly engaged environment, selling more products or services, using customised leadership tools and ecollaboration.

He has an extensive business background ranging from numerous start-up companies, large corporate environments, IT development projects and multi-nodal business enterprises. Having served many leadership roles in retail and IT, he shares his techniques and experience's with global clients. He is the author of 'Business Coach Revelations: Tips that Many Coaches and Marketing Gurus Don't Tell You!' released in April 2013.

Ron McIntyre shares articles weekly on his blog site at http://leadershipnotes.us as well as a monthly email newsletter, which you can subscribe on the blog site. His website, http://transformativeleadership.us, provides more details on his background, services and contact information. You can also find him on LinkedIn at http://www.linkedin.com/in/ronmcintyre

www.ingramcontent.com/pod-product-compliance
Lightning Source LLC
Chambersburg PA
CBHW070904180526
45168CB00005B/1926